YOUR PERFECT PET

LOVE YOUR RABBIT

Judith Heneghan

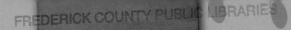

WINDMILL BOOKS
New York

Published in 2013 by Windmill Books, An Imprint of Rosen Publishing
29 East 21st Street, New York, NY 10010

Editor: Nicola Edwards
Designer: Rocket Design (East Anglia) Ltd
Picture Researcher: Nicola Edwards
Consultant: Anna Claxton

Picture Acknowledgements: The author and publisher would like to thank the following for
allowing their pictures to be reproduced in this publication:
Cover (main) Shutterstock © fivespots, (inset) iStock © Pamela Moore; title page iStock ©
Pamela Moore; p4 (tl) Shutterstock © muzsy, (tr) Shutterstock © fivespots, (b) Shutterstock
© Iakov Filimonov; p5 Shutterstock © Eric Esselée; p6 RSPCA Philip Toscano; p7 (t) Becky
Murray/RSPCA, (b) Shutterstock © Eric Esselée; p8 Shutterstock © cameilia; p9 (t) RSPCA
Andrew Forsyth, (b) Shutterstock © Kapu; p10 RSPCA Angela Hampton; p11 (t) Shutterstock ©
xjrshimada, (b) Shutterstock © Nick Biemans; p12 © Cultura Creative/Alamy; p13 (t) iStock ©
Carl Domke, (b) Shutterstock © misha shiyanov; p14 (t) Shutterstock ©AnetaPics, (b) RSPCA Joe
Murphy/RSPCA; p15 RSPCA Philip Toscano/RSPCA; p16 RSPCA David Chapman; p17 (t) RSPCA
Philip Toscano/RSPCA, (b) Shutterstock © WimL; p18 Shutterstock © foto ARts; p19 (t) iStock ©
Isabelle Mory, (b) RSPCA Chris Brignell; p20 (t) RSPCA 1093398 Andrew Forsyth/RSPCA, (b)
Shutterstock ©Dmitry Kalinovsky; p21 Shutterstock © foto Arts; p22 RSPCA Damion Diplock/
RSPCA; p23 (t) Alamy © Tierfotoagentur/Alamy, (b) Shutterstock © Alan Scheer; p24 Alamy
©Warwick Sloss/Alamy; p25 (t) Shutterstock © Eric Esselée, (b) Shutterstock © M Choco; p26
Shutterstock © Wallenrock; p27 (t) RSPCA Joe Murphy/RSPCA, (b) Shutterstock © Eric Esselée;
p28) iStock © Pamela Moore ; p29 (t) Shutterstock ©Francesco83, (b) Shutterstock © fivespots

Library of Congress Cataloging-in-Publication Data

Heneghan, Judith.
  Love your rabbit / by Judith Heneghan.
    p. cm. — (Your perfect pet)
  Includes index.
  ISBN 978-1-4777-0187-4 (library binding) — ISBN 978-1-4777-0202-4 (pbk.) —
  ISBN 978-1-4777-0203-1 (6-pack)
  1. Rabbits—Juvenile literature. I. Title.
  SF453.2.H46 2013
  636.932'2—dc23

                              2012026642

Manufactured in the United States of America

CPSIA Compliance Information: Batch #BW13WM: For Further Information contact Windmill Books, New York, New York at 1-866-478-0556

Contents

My Pet Rabbits

I have two pet rabbits named Jack and Jill. Jill is a little bigger than Jack. They are brother and sister, so they get along well. Since they are boy and girl, they have been neutered. I love watching them hop around together.

Pet rabbits need the company of other rabbits as well as their human owners.

The big question...

Can I keep just one rabbit?

Rabbits need to be with their own kind. A rabbit on its own may feel bored or stressed. If you have one, and want to introduce a friend, ask your vet for advice to make sure they don't fight. Two rabbits will need plenty of space to get away from each other if they want to.

4

Rabbits are very cute and playful, but each year thousands end up at rescue centers because their owners didn't realize how much care and attention they needed. Make sure you think carefully before choosing a rabbit for a pet. This book will help you to find out if a rabbit is the right pet for you.

Pet power

There are many types, or breeds, of pet rabbit. Different breeds vary a lot in appearance, but all pet rabbits are related to wild rabbits and show very similar behavior.

Female rabbits are called does, the males are called bucks, and their babies are called kits.

A Safe Home

Jack and Jill live outside in a special enclosure. It is big enough for them to run around and it has separate areas for sleeping, eating, and using the bathroom. It takes up quite a lot of space!

An enclosure needs to be tall enough for your rabbits to stand up on their hind legs without touching the roof.

The big question...

Can rabbits live indoors?

Some people prefer to keep their rabbits indoors. Indoor rabbits still need a shelter and plenty of room for exercise, with no access to dangers such as electric cables, poisonous plants, or other pets such as cats and dogs. They will also need somewhere to go to the bathroom, such as a tray filled with hay or newspaper.

Your rabbits need a safe and secure shelter inside their enclosure. The shelter has to be warm, dry, and big enough for your pets to lie down fully stretched out. It should also be raised off the ground to stop it from getting damp. The rabbits should to be able to move in and out of it whenever they want.

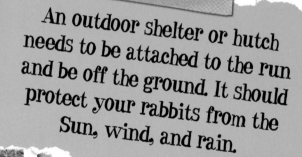

An outdoor shelter or hutch needs to be attached to the run and be off the ground. It should protect your rabbits from the Sun, wind, and rain.

Furry facts

Young rabbits reach their adult size at about five months. The rabbit shown here is five weeks old. If you buy baby rabbits, find out how big they are likely to grow and make sure your run and shelter are big enough. Two rabbits will need more space than one rabbit.

A Healthy Diet

Jack and Jill's favorite food is hay and they munch loads of it every day. They like green vegetables, too, especially broccoli and celery. Carrots are only for treats as they are more fattening. I wash the vegetables first and feed them every morning and evening.

Green vegetables form part of a healthy diet for a rabbit.

The big question...

Should I give my rabbits granola?

Rabbits are fussy eaters, so granola isn't good for them as they waste the parts they don't like. To make sure your rabbits get everything they need, give them plenty of hay and a handful of raw green vegetables every day. You can also add some good quality rabbit pellets.

Rabbits need plenty of fresh water and like to drink from a bowl. It should be heavy enough so that your rabbits won't tip it over. You could also try a water bottle with a metal spout attached to the side of the enclosure. Remember to change the water every day.

Rabbits need access to fresh water at all times.

Rabbits should have a constant supply of hay.

Pet power

Wild rabbits spend most of their time eating grass. Pet rabbits eat hay, which is dried grass. Hay needs a lot of chewing, which stops the rabbits from getting bored. It also keeps their insides and teeth healthy.

Warm and Clean

Rabbits need a warm, clean shelter for sleeping and hiding. Jack and Jill like snuggling up in a bed of fresh, dry straw. Underneath the straw there's a layer of newspaper. This makes their shelter really cozy. I change the straw and the newspaper each week.

The big question...

Why does my rabbit eat its droppings?

Grass and hay are natural foods for rabbits, but they are hard to digest. Sometimes rabbits eat their own droppings so that they pass through their bodies a second time. This is to make sure they get all the goodness they can from their food. It is quite normal and nothing to worry about.

Rabbits are very clean animals and wash their fur carefully with their tongues. They don't need a bath unless they are ill and can't clean themselves. If your rabbit looks dirty, particularly around its bottom, it may be a sign that it is unwell and you should speak to your vet.

Rabbits lick their paws and rub them over their ears to keep them clean.

Pet power

Rabbits in the wild live in underground tunnels called burrows. A burrow provides shelter from the cold and protection from larger animals such as foxes and eagles. Rabbits make sleeping nests inside the burrows, lining them with dried grass and even some of their own fur.

Wild rabbits come out of their burrow to look for food.

Holding Your Rabbit

When Jack and Jill first came to live with us, they were still young. They seemed nervous when I tried to hold them. I had to be patient until they'd learned to trust me. Now when I call their names they hop over to say hello. They don't mind being picked up, and they love it when I tickle them behind their ears!

If you spend time with your pet rabbits, they will learn to enjoy your company.

The big question...

Why does my rabbit scratch me?

If your rabbits don't like to be held, be patient. Talk quietly and try putting treats on your hand. When they trust you, they will be calmer. If you handle them, make sure their bottom is supported as they have fragile spines. All four paws should be against your body.

In the wild, rabbits are hunted by animals that are larger than them. So rabbits often feel nervous near bigger animals, like us! They won't want you holding them at first, so try sitting down next to them until they are used to your smell and your voice.

If your rabbit is nervous, use both hands to hold it in your lap while sitting on the ground. Then, if it wriggles free, it won't hurt itself.

Pet power

Rabbits have large, sensitive ears and excellent hearing. They warn other rabbits of approaching danger by thumping the ground with their back legs.

Running and Hiding

Jack and Jill are fast movers! They love hopping around their grassy run, but if they are frightened by a sudden noise or a stranger, they dash for their shelter. I've put a hollow plastic tube and an old box in the enclosure so they now have extra places to hide.

Help your rabbits feel safe by giving them lots of places to hide.

The big question...

Why does my friend's rabbit "freeze" when I go near it?

In the wild, rabbits are prey for bigger animals. Predators such as buzzards hunt them by looking for movement. So when a rabbit thinks danger is near it either runs and hides or stands completely still. If your friend's rabbit freezes, try backing away and talk gently to it so that it learns you're not a threat.

Have you ever seen a rabbit in the wild running in zigzags? If a rabbit is being chased it will try to avoid capture by quickly changing direction. Rabbits are fast and agile. Their back legs are very powerful and if danger comes too close they may use them to kick in self-defense. If your pet rabbit kicks, it may be feeling frightened.

Rabbits have strong back legs for running, leaping, and kicking.

Furry facts

Some rabbits in the wild can run at speeds of up to 45 miles per hour (72 km/h) over short distances. Pet rabbits tend to be a little slower, but they can still sprint when they want to!

Keeping Active

Jack and Jill need to dig and explore. I give them something new to investigate every week. They like logs to hop on, cardboard boxes to hide in, and balls to nudge with their noses. Jill's favorite is a hollow cardboard tube stuffed with hay. She loves to tug out the hay and eat it.

Rabbits are excellent diggers. In the wild, they live with other rabbits in a series of connected tunnels called a warren.

The big question...

Will my rabbits dig a tunnel and escape?

If your rabbits' run is outdoors, sink the frame into the ground so that they can't dig underneath the sides. However, do remember that digging is part of their natural behavior. You can help them by providing a deep tray filled with soil inside their run. Then they can dig safely!

Rabbits are intelligent animals and get bored, just like we do. To stop your rabbits from getting bored, change their toys regularly. Old toys can be put away and brought out again in a few weeks. Remember to wash them at the same time.

Whether your rabbits live outdoors or indoors, they need toys to play with and a tray for digging.

Furry facts

Rabbits see best in the dim light of dawn and dusk. This is when they are most active. However, it isn't always easy to tell if your rabbits are awake as they can sleep with their eyes open!

Fur, Teeth, and Nails

Jack and Jill have amazing teeth that never stop growing! The rough hay they chew helps grind their teeth down. I check their gums every week to make sure their teeth aren't causing problems. If a rabbit's teeth grow too long it will have a very sore mouth.

The big question...

What should I do if my rabbit's nails grow too long?

Rabbit nails should be checked regularly and may need clipping to keep them short. Get an experienced adult to do this for you.

Rabbits that live indoors on soft carpets and smooth flooring will need to have their nails clipped regularly.

Rabbits use their tongues to lick themselves clean. However, this can lead to a dangerous buildup of hair inside their stomachs. It is a good idea to groom short-haired rabbits with a soft brush once a week to remove old fur and keep their coats healthy. Long-haired rabbits will need brushing more often.

Rabbits may spend several hours a day chewing hay. This is just what their teeth need.

Furry facts

If a rabbit's teeth grow too long it can cause real suffering to the rabbit. It will probably stop eating. If you think there's a problem with your rabbit's teeth, take it to the vet for advice and treatment.

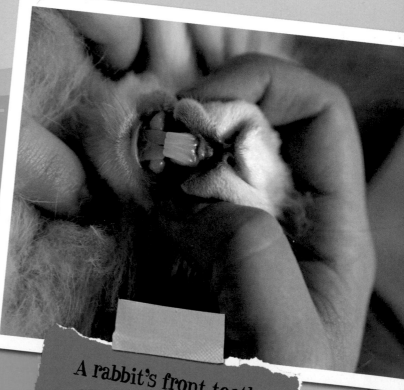

A rabbit's front teeth grow up to 0.5 inch (12 mm) every month!

Visit the Vet

We take Jack and Jill to the vet for a checkup every six months. The nurse weighs them both and the vet gives them a vaccination. Vaccinations help protect pets from dangerous diseases. I give them a treat to nibble on afterward!

A special traveling box is ideal for transporting your rabbit to the vet.

The big question...

What is neutering?

Neutering is when the vet performs an operation on your rabbit to stop it from breeding and having babies. If you have a male and a female, make sure they are neutered before you put them together.

Sick rabbits will try to hide their illness for as long as they can. In the wild, a sick rabbit is easy prey for larger animals such as foxes. So it is important to check your rabbits regularly for any signs of illness. These might include being extra sleepy, eating less than usual, drinking more than usual, having dirty fur, sticky eyes, or lumps under the skin.

A vet can give your rabbit regular checkups and tell you the best time to have it neutered.

Furry facts

If male and female rabbits aren't neutered they will soon produce a litter of up to 15 babies, or kits, and you will have to find homes for them all! Females are also more likely to develop serious illnesses if they aren't neutered.

Weather Changes

Never leave your rabbit in direct sunlight. A shady place is best.

Jack and Jill live outside in their enclosure for most of the year. In summer I make sure their shelter is in the shade to stop them from getting hot. In the winter, when it gets very cold, my dad helps me move the shelter into our garden shed.

The big question...

What is myiasis, or fly strike?
Fly strike is a very serious condition caused by flies laying their eggs in a rabbit's dirty fur. The eggs hatch into maggots which feed on the rabbit's skin. Fly strike is more likely in warm weather, so during the summer you should check daily to make sure that the fur under your rabbit's tail is clean.

If your rabbits live outside and you are worried about the cold, provide them with extra bedding or place a rug or cover over the top of their shelter. Just make sure their drinking water doesn't freeze. Or you could move their shelter into an empty shed or garage. Don't keep your rabbits in the same place as a vehicle because exhaust fumes are highly poisonous.

Make sure your rabbits have extra bedding in cold weather.

Pet power

Rabbits do not hibernate during the cold winter months, but they may slow down a little as they try to save energy. You may also notice that their fur grows more thickly.

Safety Alert!

Jack and Jill love being outdoors, but they stay in their run. Our garden isn't a safe place for rabbits to explore freely. They might hop under the gate, or eat my mom's daffodils, which would poison them. Instead we move their shelter and run around the garden so that they can experience it safely.

The big question...

My rabbits are safe from predators, aren't they?

Predators such as foxes and cats are smart creatures. They soon learn how to push through a narrow gap or lift a simple latch on a door. Make sure you lock the door of the shelter with a padlock or a metal bolt every time you close it.

If your garden is often visited by predators, bring your rabbits inside at night.

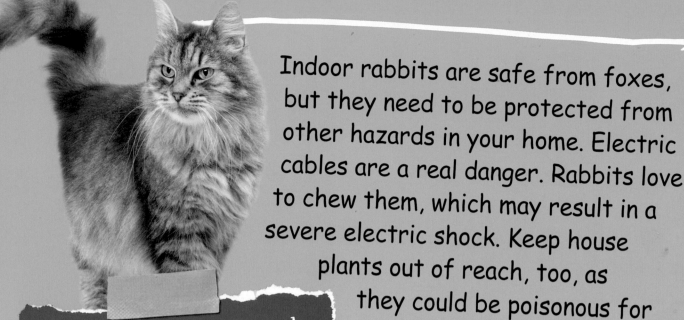

Indoor rabbits are safe from foxes, but they need to be protected from other hazards in your home. Electric cables are a real danger. Rabbits love to chew them, which may result in a severe electric shock. Keep house plants out of reach, too, as they could be poisonous for rabbits. Apple seeds are also poisonous for them.

If you have other pets, such as cats and dogs, make sure they can't scare your rabbits.

Furry facts

Plants that are poisonous for rabbits include daffodils, tulips, lily-of-the-valley, amaryllis, oleander, bracken, and most evergreen trees and shrubs. Never let your rabbit eat any unfamiliar plants.

Many common plants, such as tulips and daffodils, are poisonous for rabbits.

25

Getting Older

Jack and Jill are two years old now. They are healthy and active and I watch their diet to make sure they don't become overweight. Our vet says rabbits live longer if they stay fit and are well cared for. Older rabbits tend to slow down a little, but a balanced diet, good vet care, and a safe, fun environment will help keep them active for longer.

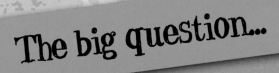

The big question...

Why is my rabbit scratching its ears so much?

Rabbits can get ear mites, which cause itching and a buildup of sticky wax and dirt. If the insides of your rabbit's ears look dirty, don't try to clean them out yourself as you may damage the sensitive inner ear. Ask your vet's advice.

If you and your family go on vacation, ask a friend or neighbor to look after your rabbits until you get back. Aim to find someone who will come to your home and look after your rabbits just as you do. However, if you need to leave your pets in someone else's home, take their shelter, their toys, and some of their old straw along as well. This will help your rabbits settle in.

If you go on vacation, leave instructions for the people who are taking care of your rabbits while you're away.

Furry facts

Pet rabbits that are well cared for can live for 8–12 years. Some can live even longer.

This rabbit is five years old. Older rabbits may be more comfortable indoors in the warmth.

Best Friends

I love my rabbits Jack and Jill. Their noses always twitch when they see me, and they've learned to come when I call their names. They need lots of care and attention, but they're worth it. We have so much fun!

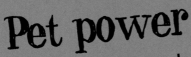

Pet power

Rabbits can be trained to do some things, such as use the bathroom in a litter box. Fill a plastic tray with torn up newspaper and place a few of your rabbit's droppings on top. Let your rabbit investigate, and reward it with a treat whenever it hops in and does its business.

My rabbits love being stroked. They are my best friends.

Rabbits communicate with each other mainly through smell. They have scent glands behind their tails and they mark their surroundings with scent as a way of leaving messages for each other. Your rabbit's nose twitches when it is trying to learn more about you.

A rabbit's whiskers are very sensitive. They help detect objects and obstacles.

Furry facts

Rabbits have an eye on each side of their head. This gives them good all-around vision for spotting bigger predator animals in the air above or behind them. It also means they have a blind spot directly in front of their noses!

Quiz

How well do you know rabbits?
Try this quick quiz to find out!

1. **Pet rabbits like to eat hay. How much should they munch each day?**
   a. A small handful
   b. As much as they like
   c. 10 pounds (4.5 kg)

2. **Rabbits have an eye on each side of the head. This means:**
   a. they can see predators behind and above them
   b. they can see two different things at once
   c. they don't have to look down their noses

3. **A rabbit's teeth never stop growing, but how quickly does this happen?**
   a. 0.5 inch (3 mm) a day
   b. 0.5 inch (3 mm) a month
   c. 0.5 inch (3 mm) a year

4. **Some plants and foods are poisonous for rabbits. Which one is poisonous here?**
   a. Broccoli
   b. Celery
   c. Apple seeds

5. **How do rabbits warn each other of approaching danger?**
   a. They thump the ground with their back legs
   b. They hop up and down
   c. They mark the ground with scent from their scent glands

6. **Why do rabbits twitch their noses?**
   a. To look cute
   b. To pick up scent from other animals
   c. To wiggle their whiskers

Answers

1(b); 2(a); 3(b); 4(c); 5(a); 6(b)

Glossary

blind spot (BLYND SPAHT) The area in front of a rabbit's nose which it can't see because of the position of its eyes.

buck (BUK) Male rabbit.

burrow (BUR-oh) A rabbit's underground home.

digest (dy-JEST) The way food is broken down inside the gut.

doe (DOH) Female rabbit.

droppings (DRAH-pingz) Animal waste.

enclosure (in-KLOH-zhur) A secure area.

environment (en-VY-ern-ment) Surroundings.

groom (GROOM) To clean and make neat.

hibernate (HY-bur-nayt) Sleep through the winter months.

hind legs (HYND LEGZ) Back legs.

hutch (HUHCH) A shelter for sleeping and keeping warm and dry.

kits (KITZ) Baby rabbits.

litter box (LIH-ter BOKS) A tray full of newspaper where rabbits can learn to use the bathroom.

neutering (NOO-ter-ing) An operation to stop a rabbit from breeding and having kits.

predator (PREH-duh-ter) An animal that hunts other animals for food.

prey (PRAY) An animal that is hunted for food.

run (RUN) A large enclosed area for outdoor exercise.

vaccination (vak-suh-NAY-shun) An injection to prevent disease.

warren (WAWR-en) An area of connecting underground burrows where lots of rabbits live.

Index

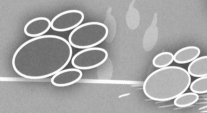

Websites

For web resources related to the subject of this book, go to:
www.windmillbooks.com/weblinks
and select this book's title.